THE LORD AND HIS LAITY

THE LORD AND HIS LAITY

David Haney

BROADMAN PRESS
Nashville, Tennessee

4255–97
ISBN: 0–8054–5597–3

Dewey Decimal Classification: 262.1
Subject heading: LAITY
Library of Congress Catalog Card Number:
78–17895
Printed in the United States of America

For the churches
who served me

Sadieville Baptist Church
Sadieville, Kentucky
 (1958–1961)

First Baptist Church
New Lebanon, Ohio
 (1962–1967)

Heritage Baptist Church
Annapolis, Maryland
 (1967–1974)

CONTENTS

THE LORD AND HIS LAITY

INTRODUCTION

Well over a decade ago, Elton Trueblood said to me that the next step in the ongoing life of the church would be a theological one. I was his student at the time, just ready to graduate from the Earlham School of Religion.

By this statement, Trueblood was saying that the resurgence of religious life then was primarily on an *experiential* level. Most revivals of religion begin there. However, this has its dangers. One danger always present is that experience can come to dictate theology rather than to be tested and tempered by it. Experience needs to be stabilized by sound theology. Revivals or awakenings invariably lift one doctrine to new heights, first by experience and then by a theological definition. The current awakening has lifted the doctrine of the "laity-as-ministers" (priesthood of the believers), and now we have reached the theological definition stage in the process, the step beyond the experiential phase.

Trueblood is not alone in his assessment. Richard Mouw, in a significant interdenominational

"Conference on the Laity" at Dallas in 1976, stated: "All this new activity . . . will ultimately fail if it has no lasting and serious theological foundation." The church must be poised, but it must also be based.

What has not been said or done, however, is that this proposed "theology of the laity" should be written *for* the laity. That which has been written, such as Kraemer's *A Theology of the Laity* and others, has been directed primarily to the clergy. Very little has been addressed to the laity itself. What has been has not seemed to fill the gap.

This book, then, is my contribution in that direction. My vantage point as the director of lay ministries has afforded me sufficient evidence to validate the need. What I have written here I have written *to the laity* and the clergy alike out of both experience and concern. My previous books *(Renew My Church, The Idea of the Laity, Breakthrough Into Renewal, Journey into Life,* and *Renewal Reminders)* have all addressed the theme from various perspectives, but in this effort I have sought to give direct attention to the biblical, theological, and historical dimensions of this next step. I have deliberately avoided theological jargon, unnecessary Greek words, quotations in Latin and German, and those other things which often frighten away or confuse the lay person. Some will assume that it is "too simplistic" I am sure. But somewhere, somehow these basic biblical and theological truths must be shared in a way in which they can be understood by our primary audience.

Several omissions are to be noted at the outset. Their omission is not to be taken as an opposition, however. It is simply that not everything can be said in a book of this size and intent. I make reference to (1) the indwelling, empowering, guiding ministry of the Holy Spirit which is necessarily a part of any study of spiritual gifts and (2) the necessity of evangelism, the obvious outgrowth of and companion to ministry. These are essential and are dealt with in detail in my previous books.

Appreciation is to be expressed to those who have aided me in this task. Encouragement and freedom to explore has come from Glendon McCullough, executive director of the Brotherhood Commission and from my immediate supervisor, Norman Godfrey. Bill Clemmons and Reid Hardin read the manuscript and made helpful suggestions. My gratitude also goes to Andrea Hawkins, my secretary, who has typed and typed. Most of all, I am in debt to my wife, Aileen, and to my children, Karen, Steve, and Philip, who walked and spoke softly while I wrote.

Now the effort is committed to Him.

David Haney

1
THE ABDICATION
OF THE LAITY

"What happened to the church in Western Europe?"

That was the question I was raising. I was in Paris, the first stop on a personal Holy-Grail search that was to take me to most of the major cities on the continent. My Grail was the answer to that question: *What happened to the church in Western Europe?*

Two hundred years ago, when the United States was emerging as a nation, Western Europe was the "center of gravity" for world Christianity. It was there that the sixteenth-century Protestant Reformation erupted and spread. It was there that the Christian thinking and writing was being done. Theology was being rewritten by their pens and in their schools. It was from there that the first missionaries of the modern missionary movement came. In fact, they were sending missionaries here to the colonies. At that time, only a small percentage of the colonists were affiliated with any church.

Now, two hundred years later, the situation

has reversed itself. The center of gravity has shifted to North America, and now in Paris and London only 5 percent of the population attends church services. In the major nations of Western Europe, church attendance is abysmally low.

What happened?

This question and its answer is all the more important as it becomes clearer and clearer that the center of gravity for world Christianity might very well be shifting out of North America. If the recent polls are valid, regular church attendance in the United States is now down to somewhere between 37 and 40 percent of the population. What is happening? Perhaps there is a lesson to be learned from the experience of Western Europe. Thus, I was there in Paris asking my question.

I first posed that question to a professor who taught in an evangelical seminary in the suburbs of Paris. He had been recommended to me by a Swiss friend who believed him to be a discerning viewer. His answer shocked me. Yet, it was the same answer, with but minor variation, that I received every time I raised the question in Europe.

I prefaced the question to him noting that Western Europe had once been the "center of gravity," yet now that center was in North America, and that attendance was down to 5 percent of the population of his city. Then, I asked:

"What happened?"

Without hesitating so much as for a breath,

he said: "The domination of the clergy!"

He went on to explain that even though the sixteenth-century Reformation had championed the "priesthood of the believer," the church had slowly but surely become redominated by the clergy. Both the clergy and the laity alike, he said, had recapitulated to what he called the "priest mentality" of pre-Reformation days.

"But why?"

His answer to this second question was even more discerning—and disconcerting. He said: "The abdication of the laity!"

Two sides to the same coin: the "domination of the clergy" and the "abdication of the laity." The clergy may dominate but only as the lay people abdicate. In short: *a ministry by default.*

The Crisis We Face

This is the crisis we face in America, in Western Europe, indeed all over the world of the church, a crisis with many dimensions and ramifications.

In Amsterdam I talked with the director of a cultural studies foundation which was funded by most of the governments and major industries in Western Europe. Their project was to ascertain the "alternative futures" available to Western Europe by A.D. 2000. When I asked how they saw the future of the church, he said without emotion: "There are some on our staff who hope *there isn't a church* by A.D. 2000!"

Jurgen Moltmann, author of *The Theology of*

Hope and one of Europe's leading theologians, says in his latest book:

> There is nothing new about the fact that the major territorial churches have today arrived at a crisis. The established churches of old do, it is true, still possess a large organization for the care of the people, with trained experts for many different ministries; but they have less and less hold on the people. *Indifference towards the church is growing; the silent falling away is spreading.* People's identification with this church is diminishing step by step. Church services are attended less and less. People are leaving the established church, in Germany because of the church tax, or for other really nonessential reasons. The church's chances of influencing society are visibly lessening. The clergy no longer feel themselves "supported" by their congregations and are often fighting a lonely battle to "get at" people. In many churches the number of new applicants for ordination no longer covers the needs of the parishes and congregations. . . . The more people are educated and the more independent they are, *the less they can put up with their merely passive role* of listener and onlooker in church services [1] (author's italics).

A crisis, and it's focus?—the domination-of-the-clergy—abdication-of-the-laity problem. As my Paris friend went on to explain, the work of *all* of the church slowly became the task of a *few* (the clergy) and the laity developed an "audience mentality." With fewer and fewer doing the work, less and less work was done. That, in turn, bred a fear—"don't rock the boat" (or perhaps we should say the "Ship of Zion") lest we lose even more members. *A church whose voice is choked by caution is soon either not heard or ignored!*

Who is to blame? Is it the domination of the clergy or is it the abdication of the laity? Who knows? I do know that most of the pastors in my acquaintance do not want to dominate. They know that authority breeds mediocrity. Yet, if they (the clergy) do not do it, who will? It is, as we said, a ministry by default.

However one views it, all facts and sides considered, the work of the church is too much of a task for but a few of its members (the clergy) no matter how gifted or how trained they may be. As one has said: "No professional clergy can do what the church is called to do." [2]

While it is true that the work of the church cannot be done by the clergy, the greater truth is that it should not be done by the clergy. Biblically, the work of the church is not the sole responsibility of the clergy; it is the task of all its members. Yet, while we may accept this in theory, in practice it is another story.

Who *is* doing the work? The pastors, of course. And they have been doing it (more by default) long enough now that some (clergy and laity alike) are assuming that it should be done by the clergy. We have simply added more clergymen, even specializing their roles, to accomplish the growing task. This was underscored for me on a subsequent trip to Europe. I was in Geneva, visiting the church which John Calvin used as the base of his Reformation activity, when I met one of its current pastors. When I asked the greatest problem they faced, both at St. Pierre's in Geneva and in Western Europe, he said: "Not enough pastors."

Not enough pastors! Yet Calvin and the other Reformers knew what the Bible teaches: there never will be "enough pastors" to do the work of the church! Our Lord, the Lord of the church, never intended for there to be. It is a task which requires *all* of the body, one which encompasses both clergy *and* laity alike.

And that is the crisis with grave effects. The absence of this biblical emphasis has led not only to the restriction of the ministry to the professional clergy but also to additional assignments which are not biblically based responsibilities of the pastor. The present-day pastor's priority list is anything but his assignment list! Most of that which he is expected to do is drawn from a model established in the rural culture of centuries passed.

The present clergyman is viewed by pulpit committees (notice the singling out of this one function, an irony in light of all that is expected in addition to his pulpit duties) as a man with a panacea for all their problems. The unspoken but statistically verifiable evidence is that they will give him two and one-half years to accomplish it. He has a program and they agree to underwrite it. He is to be the man with the answers. He is also to visit, counsel, teach, administer, build buildings, raise funds, prepare bulletins and newsletters, marry, bury, motivate, and be active in civic affairs, the local ministerium, and the denomination.

This kind of expectation means the pastor is not on tenure but on the merit system. If his preaching, programming, promoting, and personality do not produce the promised panacea— "they" know what to do! Just recently I counseled a young pastor one year out of seminary who was leaving the ministry a broken man and who had put his wife in contact with a psychiatrist. Within the same week I received a call from one pastor and a letter from another, both seeking secular employment. Called to do one thing and forced to do another, burdened with unauthorized assignments and wearied by the schedule, we are now face-to-face with truth that, as Thomas Mullen said, we have the men fit for the ministry, but not a ministry fit for the men! [3]

Add to these pastors the disillusioned laity. Raised in what one has called an "attendance-button empire," they, too, are asking: "Is this it? Is there more? There has to be more!" There is.

The Signs of Hope

Ezekiel's vision of the valley of dry bones (37:1–14) teaches a "theology of hope" for the people of God. As Gustav Weigel has said, "In every age the institutions (of religion) are dying." Yet, he continued, "they never do." [4]

In our situation, however, the signs of resurgence are definite. It is not an awakening in the traditional sense, with great crowds thronging to hear a prophet, but there is a definite and observable reemergence—a renewal.

Mark Gibbs dates this renewal as beginning in 1945. [5] He is correct. World War II was its womb. In the Axis Zone, it was focused in the efforts of Dietrich Bonhoeffer, Martin Niemöller, and others. They saw the incredible capitulation of the German church leaders, clergy and laity alike, to the Nazi ideals. They saw that the church had to be renewed—in depth, and a "confessing church" emerged though underground. Following the war, it cropped out in numerous "lay academies" in Europe, retreat centers designed to train the laity in theology and for service. Many of these are still flourishing.

On the American side, it came from the insight of both participants and observers in the war effort. On one hand, chaplains like Gordon Cosby saw the absence of the biblical, active, and contemporary faith in the lives of our Bible Belt, Sunday School products. Elton Trueblood, the Quaker philosopher, saw it as well and began to write the books which were to serve as the foundations for reconstruction in the renewal of the church. Others joined him.

On both sides, the focus was the same. Mark Gibbs said:

> In and around 1945, something rather wonderful did happen. It's partly God's answer to our prayers after the failure of the Second World War. Because of course to Christians, even a successful war is a terrible failure; and the Second World War is an enormous question mark about the whole development of Christian life in the West. In the prison camps of Germany, and of the Netherlands, in some of prison camps of Germany, and of the Allied and in the German armies, in the bombed cities of Britain and of Europe, there was a recovery of the understanding of the call of God to *all* his people, to serve him in the structures of modern society (which in that war had been so demonic), in the Monday to Saturday world. This came to us very strongly through many deep experiences of many different people, both Allied and German, and this gave us a very great prize to strive for— that in the Church of Jesus Christ, at least a considerable proportion of the laity would be just as active in their secular structures as the clergy were active in the churchly structures. That there would be a lively,

informed, alert, converted, committed, risk-
ing People of God—far more than the old
picture of the conscientious shepherd and
the rather dumb sheep.[6]

Both Bonhoeffer and Trueblood saw it and said
of it: *The renewal for which we longed lay in a
return to the laity.* Indeed, as early as 1936 Trueblood called for the "abolition of the laity" in
The Essence of Spiritual Religion, the very first
book from his pen. He said then: "The Christian
religion, especially, leads straight to the abolition
of the laity."[7]

Exactly thirty-five years later he wrote:

The rebirth of the Church, for which we
work and pray, will not come about by some
slight modification of procedure or rear-
rangement of worship patterns, however de-
sirable innovation may sometimes be. The
change must be far more profound. It will
not come by the adoption of increasingly
bizarre architecture, for that is obviously superficial. Indeed, there are indications that
the era of concentration upon the erection
of physical structures of any kind is already
over.

The profound change, which goes to the
heart of the matter, is centered on the revolutionary idea of the *ministry.*[8]

The more immediate expression of the resurgence was the emergence of "cell groups." All across the world, without any official urging, without any comparison of notes or styles, they began to appear. Small clusters of concerned, hungry believers, clergy and laity alike, began to gather in homes and apartments. They met to study, to share, to pray, and to seek both the dynamics and the places for service in the church and the world. Robert Handy in an essay in *Christianity on the March*, edited by Henry P. Van Dusen, wrote:

> An important recent development which is being felt throughout the whole church is a new emphasis on the role and place of the laity. In many places now, such phrases as "the ministry of the laity" and "the people of God" have suddenly become alive with meaning. . . .
>
> The idea that all true Christians are in some sense ministers and that the role of the ordained clergy is to minister to ministers may yet release unexpectedly powerful forces hidden within our churches.[9]

Carl Lundquist, president of Bethel College and the chairman of the Commission on Church Life for the Baptist World Alliance, recently completed a sabbatical study which took him around the world. In his unpublished study report, "The

Enduring Values of the Renewal Movement," he lists certain marks of the movement. Among them are: (1) personal allegiance to Jesus Christ; (2) devotional use of the Scriptures; (3) a rule of life [discipline]; (4) a simple life-style; (5) caring involvement with hurting people; and (6) joyous celebration.[10]

On a similar mission to Europe in 1974, this writer saw much the same.[11] All over Western Europe I stumbled onto "house churches," lay academies, churches, fellowships from churches, and clusters of groups—all centered around Bible study, sharing, prayer, discipline, caring, and ministry. The amazing thing to me was that few of these groups knew anything about the other groups, yet everywhere I went I found them— and everywhere they seemed the same. And, the underlying theorem, while not always expressed as such, was universally present: the secret to renewal in the church lays in the recovery of the New Testament concept of a gifted, ministering laity.

Michael Green similarly reports on the resurgence in South America. He says:

The growth of the Pentecostal churches (in South America) may be due to many causes, but not least is the fact that it is predominantly a *lay* church. They have, indeed, a ministry, but it is not a hierarchy. The ministers do a secular job, and they really seek to "equip the saints for the work

THE ABDICATION OF THE LAITY

of service." As a result every Christian bears
constant witness to his faith in impromptu
open-air meetings and in personal conversation with his friends. Every Christian is free
to participate in the weekly—and nightly—
meetings for worship. Doubtless these meetings are often somewhat disorderly, but they
are *alive,* because the whole people of God
take a real part. He would be a proud man
who asserted that we have nothing to learn
from them.[12]

But, as important as it is for us to know that
the churches of the New Testament era had this
concept, it is also important for us to know that
they *lost* it.

The early church had little formal organization
and the differences were those of *function,* not
position. "There were no offices with peculiar privileges, only voluntary services," according to Otto
Pfleiderer.[13] Indeed, Iraneus (A.D. 130–200) said,
"All the righteous possess the sacerdotal [priestly]
rank"; and "all disciples of the Lord are Levites
and priests."

To be sure, there were pastors, but their distinction had to do with role not rule. The clergy-
laity distinction did not exist in terms of a hierarchy, but it developed. Until then, the key to
ministry seemed to be that of the "spiritual gifts"
with which God had endowed various persons.
While the apostles were a unique group, even they
were not treated as infallible. From their Jewish

backgrounds, the early Christians developed leadership roles for "elders" (presbyters) which seemed to be inclusive of such titles as "pastor," "teacher," and "bishop." Jerome (about A.D. 420) taught that the terms *bishop* and *elder* were synonymous in the New Testament and that the later placement of the bishop *over* the elder was but an ecclesiastical arrangement.[14]

Williston Walker, the noted church historian, traces the causes of this transition to "ranks" within the church (and thus the clergy-laity gap) to the need for *authority*. He says:

> The tendencies then developed continued to work in increasing power, with the result that, between 200 and 260, the Church as an organization took on most of the constitutional features which were to characterize it throughout the period of the dominance of Graeco-Roman culture. Above all, this development was manifested in the increase of the power of the bishops. The circumstances of the time, the contests with Gnostics and Montanists, the leadership of increasing masses of ignorant recent converts from heathenism, the necessities of uniformity in worship and discipline, all tended to centralize in the bishop the rights and authority which in an earlier period had been more widely shared. The "gifts of the Spirit," which had been very real to the thought of Christians of the apostolic and subapostolic

ages, and which might be possessed by any
one, were now a tradition rather than a vital
reality.[15]

And he adds: "These 'gifts' were now the official possession of the clergy, especially of the
bishops."[16]

Kraemer, in *A Theology of the Laity,* dates the
beginning of the transition to the clergy-laity division as early as the end of the first century.[17]
But there is little doubt that by the end of the
third century it was complete. No longer was the
church a charismatic (gifted) community in which
all were ministers and all were priests, but rather
a divided group: clergy or laity, sacred or secular.
It was, as one has said, the laity *chose* what they
were to do, but the clergy were *called.* (NOTE:
The term *charismatic* used here refers, not to
"speaking in tongues," but rather to "spiritual
gifts" in general. The word *charismatic* comes
from the Greek word *charisma* or *charismata*
[plural] which literally means "gift" or "gifts."
The root of the word is the same as that of "grace"
and indicates that spiritual gifts are "gifts of
grace," meaning that these are given, not as a
result of merit or deserving, but by God's grace.
Frequently, however, the term "charismatic" is
misused to indicate "speaking in tongues." The
meaning throughout this book is that "charismatic" refers to "gifts." D. H.)

The Protestant Reformation of the sixteenth
century was to a large degree an attempt to

recover the congregational principle (as opposed to the hierarchical) and the priesthood of the believer, each the logical consequence of the other. Luther attacked it head-on. In his "Appeal to the German Nobility," he wrote: "We are all consecrated as priests by baptism, a higher consecration in us than Pope or bishop can give." [18]

But, while the reformers did recover the congregational principle, according to Moltmann, they still did not fully recover the priesthood of the believer. They grasped the principle to be sure but not the practice. It was but a "declaration of principle" and not a historical fact.[19]

Now, however, in the twentieth century, we are facing the challenge again. At the very heart of the modern renewal movement is the "ministry of the laity." To be sure, it is sometimes seen as an antichurch or an anticlergy movement, but the facts are that in the thirty years of emphasis (dating from the end of World War II), there has appeared no new denomination (centered around renewal) and the leaders of the movement have been ordained pastors. This view stems from the pressure of para-church groups which have promoted the idea rather than it coming from the institutional church.

It is helpful, however, to see that the institutional church is never an innovator. It cannot afford to be. It is the one stable factor in too many lives. Thus, when innovation comes, it usually comes from outside the institution (the official denominations) via para-church groups. A case in point is the Sunday School movement which, when it was initiated in 1780 by Robert Raikes, was actually opposed by the institutional church. Another case in point is the "youth movement." While in the 1940s few if any churches had a youth ministry, today nearly all churches, regardless of size, have either a volunteer or salaried youth director. Why? Primarily the efforts of Youth for Christ, a para-church movement (which, incidentally, gave us Billy Graham). The para-church groups serve as the research and development laboratories for the institutions, and when the problems have been worked through and the excesses toned down, the institutions adopt the changes. Thus, it is easy to see why some see these groups, at first, as antichurch simply because they challenge us at the point of business-as-usual. Lundquist says:

> As an *experimenting agency* the renewal groups are able to respond quickly to new needs as they arise. They are able to modify their structure, deploy their staff, employ new resources and allocate budgets much more quickly than churches. Often one person can make the critical decisions instead of going through a series of committees. They have their ear tuned to where people hurt more than to what bureaucracies have prioritized. They are quickly aware of what is being attempted by sister groups. They can afford to try new forms with less risk.
> It seems to me that these groups ought

to be encouraged to experiment on behalf
of the whole church. Then the proven new
ministries often can be incorporated into the
life of the church to enrich its work for
God.[20]

Some see the current movement in its return
to the New Testament concept of the ministering
laity as an anticlergy thrust. But, as Colin Williams notes:

> The experience of the centuries is that
> abolition of clerics is no cure of clericalism.
> Soon leaders emerge again from the commu-
> nity who assume the same traditional
> roles . . . .
> Such a ministry is required to carry re-
> sponsibility for the apostolic faith and to
> order the training of the laity for their
> ministry.[21]

It is not the clergy but clericalism which is
the issue—the *exclusivism* of the ministry.

As in the New Testament and subsequent eras,
there is a fear today of the abuse of gifts. To be
sure, they can be (and are) abused as they were
in the church at Corinth (see 1 Cor. 14). But it
is the very situation of hierarchy which prompts
the abuse! Moltmann says:

> Whenever the church loses this justifica-
> tion, this experience and this perspective, the

diversity of the charismata and the unity of the charismatic community is lost. Then hierarchies and monarchical episcopates grow up on the one hand, and merely passive church members, incapable of independent decision and action, on the other. This is when apathy develops and outbreaks of "enthusiasm" take place.[22]

Moltmann adds, however, that "there are a great many churches and congregations today which are anything but threatened by enthusiasm!"[23] He concludes: "The traditional fear of a chaos of spiritual gifts is, in the face of their present poverty, without foundation.[24]

"In face of their present poverty!" That is the signal. It is our present poverty which demands that we risk and that we return to the New Testament way of ministry. We must move beyond the *excesses* (the answer does not lie there) to the *essence:* the ministry of the body, the whole body. As Kraemer said:

A new manifestation of the real nature and calling of the Church, in power and spirit, is demanded; not simply a restoration of the Church, or a Church more active in more directions than ever. The world unconsciously waits for the appearance of the Church in its true nature. *Renewal* of the Church is therefore the indispensable element.[25]

2
THE VOCATION
OF THE CHRISTIAN

What does the word *laity* mean? It simply means "the people" and, in the Christian sense, the "people of God." Originally, when applied to Christians, it referred to all of the people of God. This was also true of a word *clergy* which comes from the root word *kaleo,* meaning "to call." The word *vocation* comes from the Latin word *vocatio,* meaning "to call." Originally, it was understood that all of the people of God were "called." There is nothing in either word to distinguish one believer from another.

But, the Christian movement was barely one hundred years old when "clergy" and "laity" took a turn in meaning. Thus, Clement of Rome used "laity" to refer to the ordinary membership in his letter to the Corinthians (A.D. 95) and followed the introduction of the term with the first known reference and presentation of rank within the church.[1] Since then the gap has only widened. It is now an established hierarchial designation.

Change, however, is coming. A part of the mod-

ern renewal movement's thrust has been a return
to the Scriptures, and now we are returning to
the biblical definitions: the "people of God" who
are the "called of God." It is clergy-laity not
clergy *and* laity. And, as we renew the proper
usage of the terms, we are coming to see that
the definitions are not limited to *who*, but that
they also include *what* the people of God are to
do.

The Metaphors of the Laity

There are three primary New Testament metaphors (word pictures) for the people of God which
relate to both who they are and what they do.
One is a *relational* term, another is a *spiritual*
term, and the other is *functional*.[2]

The relational metaphor: the *bride*. This term,
the bride or the bride of Christ, speaks of the
kind of deep and meaningful love which exists
between Christ and his followers—a relationship.
Its primary thrust is *who* we are in relationship
to him. This nuptial theme appears in the teachings of John the Baptist (John 3:25–29), in the
teachings of Jesus (Mark 2:18–20), in John (Rev.
19:7–9), and Paul (1 and 2 Cor.).[3]

The spiritual metaphor: the *temple*. As Paul
wrote in 2 Corinthians 6:16, "We are the temple
of the living God" (RSV). In 1 Corinthians 6:19f,
"We are the temple of the Holy Spirit." It has
a spiritual meaning. That is, God dwells not in
a building but in his people. Thus Paul wrote:

You are no longer aliens in a foreign land, but fellow-citizens with God's people, members of God's household. You are built upon the foundation laid by the apostles and prophets, and Christ Jesus himself is the foundation-stone. In him the whole building is bonded together and grows into a holy temple in the Lord (Eph. 2:19–21, NEB).

The functional metaphor: the *body*. This is the more widely used term and its stress has to do with the function of the people of God. A body functions. With Christ as its head (Col. 1:18; 2:19), the body works together. As Paul expressed it:

Just as in a single human body there are many limbs and organs, all with different functions, so all of us, united with Christ, form one body, serving individually as limbs and organs to one another (Rom. 12:4–5, NEB).

And in greater detail:

A body is not one single organ, but many. Suppose the foot should say, "Because I am not a hand, I do not belong to the body," it does belong to the body none the less. Suppose the ear were to say, "Because I am not an eye, I do not belong to the body," it does still belong to the body. If the body were all eye, how could it hear? if the body were all ear, how could it smell? But, in fact, God appointed each limb and organ to its own place in the body, as he chose. If the whole were one single organ, there would not be a body at all; in fact, however, there are many different organs, but one body. The eye cannot say to the hand, "I do not need you"; nor the head to the feet, "I do not need you." Quite the contrary; those organs of the body which seem to be more frail than others are indispensable, and those parts of the body which we regard as less honourable are treated with special honour. To our unseemly parts is given a more than ordinary seemliness, whereas our seemly parts need no adorning. But God has combined the various parts of the body, giving special honour to the humbler parts, so that there might be no sense of division in the body, but that all its organs might feel the same concern for one another. If one organ suffers, they all suffer together. If one flourishes, they all rejoice together (1 Cor. 12:14–26, NEB).

While these three metaphors must be held in balance, it is in the functional that the clearest definition of laity is found because it tells what the laity is to do in light of the spiritual and relational dimensions. Because the people of God are in a love relationship to Christ and because they are indwelt by his Spirit, they are *to do* certain things.

The Functions of the Body

In both Ephesians and 1 Corinthians, as Paul deals with the body concept, he invariably links it to the ideas of (1) spiritual gifts, (2) the calling of God, and (3) the ministry. The ideas interlock: as the body functions, it does so because its members are gifted and called to ministry. Note in each of the following passages how the terms are linked:

1 Corinthians 12:4–13, NEB

There are varieties of gifts, but the same Spirit. There are varieties of service, but the same Lord. There are many forms of work, but all of them, in all men, are the work of the same God. In each of us the Spirit is manifested in one particular way, for some useful purpose. One man, through the Spirit, has the gift of wise speech, while another, by the power of the same Spirit, can put the deepest knowledge into words. Another, by the same Spirit, is granted faith; another, by the one Spirit, gifts of healing, and another miraculous powers; another has the gift of prophecy, and another ability to distinguish true spirits from false; yet another has the gift of ecstatic utterance of different kinds, and another the ability to interpret it. But all these gifts are the work of one and the same Spirit, distributing them separately to each individual at will. For Christ is like a single body with its many limbs and organs, which, many as they are, together make up one body. For indeed we were all brought into one body by the baptism, in the one Spirit, whether we are Jews or Greeks, whether slaves or free men, and that one Holy Spirit was poured out for all of us to drink.

Romans 12:4–8, NEB

Just as in a single human body there are many limbs and organs, all with different functions, so all of us, united with Christ, form one body, serving individually as limbs and organs to one another. The gifts we possess differ as they are allotted to us by God's grace, and must be exercised accordingly: the gift of inspired utterance, for example, in proportion to a man's faith; or the gift of administration, in administration. A teacher should employ his gift in teaching, and one who has the gift of stirring speech should use it to stir his hearers. If you give to charity, give with all your heart; if you are a leader, exert yourself to lead; if you are helping others in distress, do it cheerfully.

Ephesians 4:1–16, NEB

I entreat you, then—I, a prisoner for the Lord's sake: as God has called you, live up to your calling. Be humble always and gentle, and patient too. Be forebearing with one another and charitable. Spare no effort to make fast with bonds of peace the unity which the Spirit gives. There is one body and one Spirit, as there is also one hope held out in God's *call* to you; one Lord, one faith, one baptism; one God and Father of all, who is over all and through all and in all. But each of us has been given his gift, his due portion of Christ's bounty. Therefore Scripture says:

"He ascended into the heights with captives in his train; he gave gifts to men."

Now, the word "ascended" implies that he also descended to the lowest level, down to the very earth. He who descended is no other than he who ascended far above all heavens, so that he might fill the universe. And these were his gifts: some to be apostles, some prophets, some evangelists, some pastors and teachers, *to equip God's people for work in his service,* to the building up of the body of Christ. So shall we all at last attain to the unity inherent, in our faith and our knowledge of the Son of God—to mature manhood, measured by nothing less than the full stature of Christ. We are no longer to be children, tossed by the waves and whirled

about by every fresh gust of teaching, dupes
of crafty rouges and their deceitful schemes.
No, let us speak the truth in love; so shall
we fully grow up into Christ. He is the head,
and on him the whole body depends. Bonded
and knit together by every constituent joint,
the whole frame grows through the due activity of each part, and builds itself up in
love (Author's italics).

What does this say? It says that . . .

All Believers Are Called. No longer can we
accurately say that "calling" is the designation
for a few: pastors, missionaries, the clergy. *All*
God's children are called. As Moltmann says:

> The community of the baptized is the
> community of those who have been called.
> There are no differences here. All are called
> and commissioned for eternal life, the glory
> of the kingdom and messianic fellowship,
> charged to live in the messianic presence of
> this eschatological future and to bear witness
> to it. That becomes especially clear when
> we enquire into priesthood in the New Testa-
> ment. When the New Testament uses the
> word "priest" it does not mean any special
> priestly class.[4]

One of the callings is that of "pastor," but the
calling does not have to do with *position* as much
as it does to *function* (see chap. 3). It also means
that . . .

All Believers Are Gifted. No longer may we validly speak of a certain few as being gifted to the exclusion of the whole body—for the whole body is gifted. The Greek word for gift is *charisma* and it has the same root as the word *grace*. It denotes a gift freely given to one by another totally apart from merit or worth. And Paul says: "Each of us has been given his gift" (Eph. 4:7, NEB).

In various passages, Paul lists representative gifts by way of illustration. By no means did Paul intend to limit the number of gifts to those he listed, as some would have us to believe. In each list Paul gives different functions, not exact categories.

Kenneth Gangel lists these gifts in alphabetical order as follows:

1. Administration
2. Apostleship
3. Discernment
4. Evangelism
5. Exhortation
6. Faith
7. Giving
8. Healings
9. Interpretation
10. Knowledge
11. Mercy
12. Miracles
13. Ministering
14. Pastoring
15. Prophecy

16. Teaching
17. Tongues
18. Wisdom [5]

The various functions of the members of the body draw upon these gifts for fulfillment. They are not the exclusive property of any one member. "The widow who exercises mercy is acting just as charismatically as a 'bishop.' " [6]

And, it means that . . .

All Believers Are Ministers. As one has expressed it: "Some of my friends are ministers and a few of them are ordained." The word *minister* is the translation of the Greek word *diakonia* from which we get our word *deacon*. It means "servant." The root of the word is *eukoneo* which means "eager" and indicates an eagerness to serve. Our current interpretation (not definition) is that it refers only to those who are ordained. Yet the renewal of the New Testament terminology is coming to pass. Indeed it must. As S. A. Newman says:

> A ministry of "servants," recognized for the services they rendered rather than for the position they occupied, represents the purest form of the ministry in the early church. This is the only form of ministry which is consonant with the essential character of Christian faith.[7]

All believers are called; all believers are gifted;

all believers are ministers. That is the New Testament theology of the laity and the clergy.

The New Testament knows no technical term for what we call "the church's ministry." Paul talks about charismata, meaning the energies of the new life (1 Cor. 12:6,11), which is to say the powers of the Spirit. These are designations of what is, not of what ought to be. They are the gifts of grace springing from the creative grace of God. When he talks about the use of these new living energies, on the other hand, he evidently avoids all the words expressing conditions of rule. He does not talk about "holy rule" (hierarchy) but chooses the expression *diakonia*. Creative grace leads to new obedience; and the gifts of grace and the energies of the Spirit lead to ready, courteous service. Claims and privileges cannot be deduced from them. The source of life's new forces is the new life itself. "The charisma of God is eternal life in Christ Jesus our Lord" (Rom. 6:23). Just as the new life becomes manifest and efficacious in life's new powers, so the eschatological gift of the Holy Spirit also becomes manifest and efficacious in the powers of the Spirit. The charismata can be understood as the crystallization and individuation of the one charis given in Christ. Through the powers of the Spirit, the one Spirit gives every individual his specific share and calling, which is exactly cut out for him, in the process of the new creation.[8]

The Evidence of the Early Church

The evidence of this is to be seen in the life and life-style of the early church at three points. First, they were a *koinonia,* a fellowship, which simply transcended any discussion of rank or position. They held all things in common—which included the ministry. Philip and Stephen, lay deacons, also preached (Acts 6; 8). Ananias, a layman, laid hands on Saul of Tarsus both healing and commissioning him (Acts 9). Aquila and Priscilla were lay missionaries (Acts 18). And on and on.

Second, and equally important, is the awareness that while Paul wrote to a number of congregations, none of those particular letters were addressed to a pastor. Paul wrote letters to the churches at Rome, Corinth, Ephesus, Philippi, Colosse, Thessalonica, and a circulating letter to the churches of Galatia. Yet not one of them was addressed to the pastor! In fact, even after reading the letter, one is hard put to discover who the pastor was!

What does this say about the nature of the New Testament churches? That they had no pastors? I doubt that. There is too much emphasis in the Epistles on the role of the pastor. What, then, does it say?

Whatever else, it says that the work of the

church was not solely the responsibility of the pastor. Whoever he was, he was but one among the others in the body. Every member of the body has his or her own ministry. The pastor's role was to equip the laity for their ministries (see Eph. 4:11–12). Consequently, Paul's letters were addressed to the congregation—which included the pastor, not to the pastor for the congregation.

Third, while we have no accounts of actual worship services in the New Testament, there is an indication in 1 Corinthians that they were to great degree lay led. In 1 Corinthians 14, as Paul deals with the abuse of tongues, there is a reference to worship.

> To sum up, my friends: when you meet for worship, each of you contributes a hymn, some instruction, a revelation, an ecstatic utterance, or the interpretation of such an utterance. All of these must aim at one thing: to build up the church (1 Cor. 14:26–27, NEB).

There was obviously an air of spontaneity to their worship and, more importantly, an openness to lay participation. Evidently, it was not clergy dominated.

What does all of this mean? It means that every believer has his or her own gift (or gifts), clergy and laity alike. Each has been called and each has his or her own ministry. No longer can any hide behind that cloak of self-righteous humility which says, "There are some who are gifted, but I'm not one of them." Not so!

It means that the ministry of the church must be a shared ministry. The pastor is to "equip the saints for the work of the ministry" (Eph. 4:11–12, KJV); that is his ministry. He is to help them discover their gifts; to grasp the various ministries through which that gift may enable them to serve; and to educate, to enable, and to encourage them in their callings.

Only with this style of shared ministry in which we once again see the genius and the planning of our Lord can we ever reach the world. It will be a return to the priesthood of all believers; indeed, a return to the New Testament. As Trueblood said: "Here was a new order; the old system was overcome, not by destroying its priesthood, but by enlarging it to incude all devout souls." [9]

3
THE VALIDATION
OF THE CLERGY

Does all of this do away with the need for pastors? If the laity are ministers, what is *the* minister to do? Nothing is of greater concern in the church today than the role and function of the ordained leadership. And rightly so for it is at the center of our challenge today.

What Is the Pastor Doing?

Some would say that today's pastor is doing everything but that for which he was gifted and called to do—either by choice or by the coercion of circumstances. Of this, one has observed:

> The clergyman's abiding frustration is that in doing the many things that are useful, he may be prevented from doing the one thing needful. It is being suggested here that the one thing needful in the role of the clergyman for our time is that he prepare his people for their ministry in the church and in the world. *The chief task of the clergyman*

57

is to equip his people for their ministry. All his work is to this end. The functions of preacher, prophet, pastor, priest, evangelist, counselor, and administrator find their proper places in the equipping ministry. The purpose of this ministry is that the people shall be trained and outfitted for their work in the church and in the world.[1]

A good many of those things which the pastor is having to do today have little or nothing to do with his gifts or calling. These duties have just accumulated across the years, mostly culturally induced, and some of those duties have been around long enough now that many people merely assume that these tasks are a part of his assignment from God. Of course, this has created many problems not the least of which is a massive ministerial desertion problem. But, there is a greater problem—a challenge—and it has to do with the following question.

What *Should* the Pastor Do?

What is the role, the function of the pastor? Surprisingly enough, there are very few passages in the New Testament which deal with what the pastor is to do. Indeed, the emphasis of those passages is on what he is *to be* as a *person,* rather than what he is *to do* as a *pastor.*

Key Passages. There are three key passages on the role of the pastor, on his qualifications, and on his functions: 1 Timothy 3:1–7; Titus 1:5–9; and 2 Timothy 2:22–24.

There is a popular saying: "To aspire to leadership is an honourable ambition." Our leader, therefore, or bishop, must be above reproach, faithful to his one wife, sober, temperate, courteous, hospitable, and a good teacher; he must not be given to drink, or a brawler, but of a forbearing disposition, avoiding quarrels, and no lover of money. He must be one who manages his own household well and wins obedience from his children, and a man of the highest principles. If a man does not know how to control his own family, how can he look after a congregation of God's people? He must not be a convert newly baptized, for fear the sin of conceit should bring upon him a judgement contrived by the devil. He must moreover have a good reputation with the non-Christian public, so that he may not be exposed to scandal and get caught in the devil's snare (1 Tim. 3:1–7, NEB).

My intention in leaving you behind in Crete was that you should set in order what was left over, and in particular should institute elders in each town. In doing so, observe the tests I prescribed: is he a man of unimpeachable character, faithful to his one wife, the father of children who are believers, who are under no imputation of loose living, and

are not out of control? For as God's steward
a bishop must be a man of unimpeachable
character. He must not be overbearing or
short-tempered; he must be no drinker, no
brawler, no money-grabber, but hospitable,
right-minded, temperate, just, devout, and
self-controlled. He must adhere to the doctrine, so that he may be well able both to
move his hearers with wholesome teaching
and to confute objectors (Titus 1:5–9 NEB).

Turn from the wayward impulses of
youth, and pursue justice, integrity, love,
and peace with all who invoke the Lord in
singleness of mind. Have nothing to do with
foolish and ignorant speculations. You know
they breed quarrels, and the servant of the
Lord must not be quarrelsome, but kindly
towards all (2 Tim. 2:22–24, NEB).

In each of the above, the emphasis is on the
kind of person a pastor (or elder or servant of
the Lord) is to be. (Let it be understood, too,
that these hold true as expectations of any and
all believers; there is no double standard for Christian behavior.) The lists are very similar: he must
be a gentleman, even tempered, hospitable, a vic-
tor over drink and money, devout, of a good reputation (pays his bills and keeps his word), a family
man, and so on.

But, what is he *to do?* The one common and
distinguishing element in each of these passages

is that the pastor is *to teach*. It is the one thing, the only thing mentioned, that he is to do. All of the other requirements have to do with what the pastor is to be, and they hold true for any other believer!

In 1 Timothy 3:1–7, he is to be "a good teacher" ("with a gift for teaching," Weymouth translation).

In Titus 1:9, NEB, he is to "move his hearers with wholesome teaching" ("able to give instruction," RSV).

In 2 Timothy 2:22–24, he should be a "good teacher" ("a skillful teacher," Williams translation.)

Also, in two of the three above passages, there is an emphasis on discipline: he is a discipliner as a father to his children (1 Tim. 3:4–5), and he is to be gentle when exercising it (2 Tim. 2:24). The word *discipline* is from the word *disciple* which means "learner." It is "corrective teaching" but teaching nonetheless.

Thus, teaching is his distinguishing mark, his gift, according to these key passages.

Pastoral Epistles. The above passages, written to actual pastors, are in only three letters which are contained in the New Testament canon. Thus, they are extremely important in determining the role of the pastor. Beyond those passages which specifically deal with the office, there are interesting sidelights. What does Paul tell Timothy and Titus to do? Beyond the qualifications of pastors in general, what does Paul say to Timothy and to Titus, personally, in these letters? Notice what he says:

> By offering such advice as this to the brotherhood you will prove a good servant of Christ Jesus, bred in the precepts of our faith and of the sound instruction which you have followed (1 Tim. 4:6, NEB).

> Pass on these orders and these *teachings*. Let no one slight you because you are young, but *make yourself an example* to believers in speech and behaviour, in love, fidelity, and purity. Until I arrive devote your attention to the public reading of the scriptures, to exhortation, and to teaching (vv. 11–13, NEB).

> Perserve in them, keeping close watch on yourself and your *teaching;* by doing so you will further the salvation of yourself and your hearers (v. 16, NEB).

> Elders who do well as leaders should be reckoned worthy of a double stipened, in particular those who labour at *preaching* and *teaching* (5:17, NEB).

> This is what you are to *teach* and *preach* (6:3, NEB).

> *Instruct* those who are rich in this world's goods not to be proud (v. 17, NEB).

> *Tell* them to do good and to grow rich in noble actions, to be ready to give away and to share (v. 18, NEB).

Of this Gospel I, by his appointment, am herald, apostle, and *teacher* (2 Tim. 1:11, NEB).

Keep before you an outline of the sound *teaching* (v. 13, NEB).

Now therefore, my son, take strength from the grace of God which is ours in Christ Jesus. You heard my *teaching* in the presence of many witnesses; put that *teaching* into the charge of men you can trust, such men as will be competent to *teach* others (2:1–2, NEB).

Go on reminding people of this, and charge them solemnly before God to stop disputing about mere words; it does no good, and is the ruin of those who listen. Try hard to show yourself worthy of God's approval, as a labourer who need not be ashamed; be straightforward in your *proclamation* of the truth (vv. 14–15, NEB).

Before God, and before Christ Jesus who is to judge men living and dead, I charge you solemnly by his coming appearance and his reign, *proclaim the message,* press it home on all occasions, convenient or inconvenient, use argument, reproof, and appeal, with all the patience that the work of *teaching* requires. For the time will come when they will not stand wholesome *teaching,* but will follow their own fancy and gather a crowd of teachers to tickle their ears. They will stop their ears to the truth and turn to mythology. But you yourself must keep calm and sane at all times; face hardship, work to spread the Gospel, and do all the duties of your calling (4:1–5, NEB).

For your own part, what you say must be in keeping with wholesome *doctrine* (Titus 2:1, NEB).

Urge the younger men, similarly, to be temperate in all things, and set them a good example yourself. In your *teaching,* you must show integrity and high principle, and use wholesome speech to which none can take exception (vv. 6–7, NEB).

These, then, are your *themes;* urge them and argue them. And speak with authority: let no one slight you (v. 15, NEB).

Remind them to be submissive (3:1, NEB).

Our own people must be *taught* to engage in honest employment to produce the necessities of life; they must not be unproductive (v. 14, NEB).

It hardly needs to be said for it is so clear: *teach!*

The Ephesian Passage. The reference in Ephesians 4: 1–16 is important in that it is the passage which speaks of the pastor as a gift. Other passages deal with the gifts of the pastor—those special, supernatural abilities which he uses in the performances of his duties. But the reference in Ephesians states that the pastor himself is a gift, God's gift to the body.

Notice several facets of this important passage. First, Paul mentions "calling" (vv. 1,4). Since it is a letter to the church, it is to be assumed that the laity are included among the called.

Second, he stresses that the laity is involved in being gifted, also (v. 7).

The thrust of this inclusion of the laity is to be seen in verses 5–6: God is over all, through all, and in all.

Third, as he deals with gifts, Paul speaks of them as being "apostles," "prophets," "evangelists" (v. 11), and, then, as "pastors and teachers." Notice how he links the two: pastors *and* teachers (v. 11). The pastor's role, he continues, is "to equip God's people for work in his service." In other translations, this is rendered "for the work of the ministry." (In some translations there is a comma between "to equip God's people" and "for the work of the ministry." However, in the Greek language, there are no punctuation marks, hence the placement of that comma was a translator's choice—and error. It is not two thoughts, but one: "to equip for ministry.")

Thus, again, the pastor's role is presented: to teach.

Other Related Passages. There are three other related passages with a bearing on the biblical function of the pastor. The first is: "Remember your leaders, those who first spoke God's message to you; and reflecting upon the outcome of their life and work, follow the example of their faith" (Heb. 13:7, NEB).

The pastor is to be an example. What does an example do? It teaches by way of illustration. The second is:

> I appeal to the elders of your community, as a fellow-elder and a witness of Christ's sufferings, and also a partaker in the splendour that is to be revealed. Tend that flock of God whose shepherds you are, and do it, not under compulsion, but of your own free will, as God would have it; not for gain but out of sheer devotion; not tyrannizing over those who are allotted to your care, but setting an example to the flock. And then, when the Head Shepherd appears, you will receive for your own the unfading garland of glory.
>
> In the same way you younger men must be subordinate to your elders. Indeed, all of you should wrap yourselves in the garment of humility towards each other, because God sets his face against the arrogant but favours the humble (1 Pet. 5:1–5, NEB).

The elders are to tend the flock of God as a shepherd (v. 2) by setting an example (v. 4). Again, the teaching role.

Finally, the classic passage:

> During this period, when disciples were growing in number, there was disagreement between those of them who spoke Greek and

those who spoke the language of the Jews. The former party complained that their widows were being overlooked in the daily distribution. So the Twelve called the whole body of disciples together and said, "It would be a grave mistake for us to neglect the word of God in order to wait at table. Therefore, friends, look out seven men of good reputation from your number, men full of the Spirit and of wisdom, and we will appoint them to deal with these matters, while we devote ourselves to prayer and to the ministry of the Word" (Acts 6:1–4, NEB).

Why was lay assistance necessary? So that the apostles might give themselves "to prayer and the ministry of the Word" (v. 4).

In every passage in the New Testament which refers to the pastoral role, the exclusive emphasis is to teach—by word of proclamation, by instruction, with example, and through discipline. To teach!

Bishops, Elders, Pastors. These three terms or titles are the most often used in the New Testament to designate the pastoral role. "Pastor" is used but once in this official functional sense, in Ephesians 4, and then it is linked to "teachers." The word itself means "shepherd."

"Bishop" and "elder" are more frequently used. The term *bishop* means "overseer." The word is transliterated from the Greek as *episkopos* from

which we get the English "episcopal." Scholars
are agreed that it has no Jewish prototype or ante-
cedent. However, "elder" does. Most scholars believe that the early church drew on the Jewish
system of "elders" for this role. Their Old Testament function was primarily that of (1) the interpretation of doctrine and (2) the discipline of
those who erred from it.[2] It was a teaching function.

What is interesting is that the New Testament
coidentifies these two terms, bishop and elders.
J. B. Lightfoot holds that they are synonyms. The
idea that these were ranked offices, one above the
other, came much later as the church borrowed
an administrative life-style from Roman monarchical government. In Acts 20, Paul called for
a meeting of the Ephesian elders (v. 17). However,
as he addressed them, he called them bishops (v.
28) which *The New English Bible* translates as
shepherds (pastors). The evidence is that the terms
were viewed as synonyms and that the primary
emphasis was on the teaching role. Thus, Paul
admonishes these Ephesian elders-bishops-pas-
tors:

> I know that when I am gone, savage
> wolves will come in among you and will not
> spare the flock. Even from your own body
> there will be men coming forward who will
> distort the truth to induce the disciples to
> break away and follow them. So be on the
> alert; remember how for three years, night

and day, I never ceased to counsel each of you, and how I wept over you (Acts 20:29–31, NEB).

Notice that their function had to do with the correction of distorted truth: again, the teaching role.

What Does This Mean?

Whatever else it means, there need be no question about the New Testament concept of the pastor's role. Regardless of the duties the church has added across the centuries, whether validly or invalidly, the pastor is to teach, first and foremost. His leadership, tending the flock of God, is based upon his authority as a teacher of the Way. And, what is he to teach? Those things which will "equip the saints for the work of the ministry."

This has implications for the clergy and the laity alike. For the clergy, it requires an understanding of and a return to this New Testament function. For the laity, it demands a release, a release of their pastors from those duties which hinder their true work. If the pastors are to equip the saints, the saints are to release the pastors to do it!

4
THE ACTIVATION OF
THE CHURCH

What are the implications of the lay ministry for the local bodies of Christ? If we can and do rediscover the New Testament concept, how then is it implemented? Dr. James Mahoney in *Journey Into Usefulness* lists six axioms for such a church.

Axiom # 1—The church is to function as one body with many members (1 Cor. 12:12,17).

Axiom # 2—The Holy Spirit provides each member with a gift (enabling) to fulfill a particular service in and through the body for the profit of all (vv. 4,7). Each member is to major in that area as his basic ministry.

Axiom # 3—The body's activity is equal to the various functions of its members, nothing more (vv. 15–17).

Axiom # 4—Each member's function is vital to the body . . . and he should serve in that capacity (vv. 18–21).

Axiom # 5—God leads each member to a function by which he can best execute his spiritual gift in and through the body (vv. 18,28).

Axiom # 6—The church staff and training force are to equip each member for his function (1 Cor. 12:18,28; Eph. 4:12, a companion passage).

To each of his axioms, he adds certain corresponding implications or stratagems.

Stratagem 1—Each member of the church is a minister but should serve in unity with fellow members.

Stratagem 2—The church teaching program must fully enlighten each member of the privilege and responsibility of exercising his gift.

Stratagem 3—Any church function that cannot be maintained without constant pastoral pressure upon the people, should be allowed to die a natural death (Robert Girard).

Stratagem 4—A member should not be fulfilling a major function for which he is not gifted.

Stratagem 5—The church nominating committee must recognize a mem-

ber's gift and function, then
fit the program to him . . .
rather than determine the
program, then seek individu-
als to staff it.

Stratagem 6—The true effectiveness of a
church, in terms of service,
will equal the ability of its
training force to help each
member develop and execute
his spiritual gift . . . and fulfill his redemptive mission in
this world.[2]

But, how does a church get there? How does
a church arrive at these axioms and stratagems?
How does a church begin to act like this New
Testament view? Lloyd Ogilvie suggests the raising of four questions to ascertain a valid direction:
What kind of lay person are we trying to deploy
in the world? What kind of church deploys that
kind of lay person? What kind of official board
makes possible that kind of church? And what
kind of clergy does it require?

Catching the Vision

It is obvious that the congregation must see
the vision of the church through the eyes of
Christ. They must grasp the theology of it—or
be grasped by it. They must begin to examine,
to explore, and to experiment. All of which means

that the pastor must see it first. He must grasp
the theology of it and be grasped by it. And, above
all, he must be willing to examine and explore
and experiment with it.

Happily, however, the pastor is not without
resources. Much of the experimentation has taken
place, and the problems have been worked
through. Not only is this the case in the realm
of the church, but in the secular world as well.
Bruce Larson has discovered the idea of lay leadership is gaining support in most of the helping professions via para-professionals. He reports:

> Most of the helping professions already
> make extensive use of volunteers and non-
> professionals. This is not new. What is new
> in our time is the growing awareness that
> in some cases the paraprofessional or non-
> professional is better able to do the job than
> the professional. The idea must be aban-
> doned that we are using amateurs or para-
> professionals because "the real thing" is not
> available. Rather, from studies made in
> many fields, there is a weight of evidence
> that the professionals have been largely
> ineffective.[3]

The evidence of its workability within the
church abounds. But, the pastor, as the leader,
is the conveyor of this vision to the congregation.
As the administrative leader, he is the one who

can structure for it, enable it, and allow it to be. Thus he begins to fulfill his role as teacher and "equipper" of the saints.

Keeping the Good

This renewal of the New Testament church concept does not require jettisoning the whole of our present structures and programs. There are certain essentials which must be maintained and even strengthened. Moltmann says that these essentials are *kerygma* (proclaiming), *koinonia* (fellowship), and *diakonia* (ministry or service).[4] Proclaiming the gospel, loving each other, and ministering in Christ are indeed "musts." And we must keep on doing them—worshiping, educating, training, discipling, giving, supporting missions, and all the other things we are collectively called to do. These things make for a complete lay person. While the lay person is a minister, these are those things which equip and strengthen. They are integral to ministry.

This does not, however, mean that the present methods of doing these things are the best possible ways. These must be constantly evaluated and updated for effectiveness.

Education and training, for instance, must be viewed from a new perspective: Do our educational programs actually equip persons for their ministry? Is the education tied to what persons are to do, or is it merely to know?

Concerning worship, James Mahoney says:

The church must come around to altering its form of worship. The worship service must be made conducive to lay participation. If the laity are to be personally engaged in such activities as prophecy, exhortation, evangelizing, and be free to seek God for miracles and healing . . . they must be *drawn in* and *turned on!* . . .

Laymen must be "drawn in" to increased participation in our worship services. Inject dialogue. Encourage spontaneous testimony as a means of exhortation. Insert a prayer-for-healing time. Use laymen to read the Scriptures and counsel those who wish to seek God. Allow laymen to preach, sing, promote and instruct. . . .

Laymen must be drawn in, but they must also be "turned on." Too often our worship services are "locked in" to a set pattern. Each hymn, announcement period, and Scripture reading have their accustomed place in the printed program, from which we never deviate. But we acclimate our worship services. Allow time for people to be more relaxed and expressive. Occasionally pull the anthems down lower. Sift out some ritual and sing the contemporary. Encourage congregational singing and open up for times of earnest prayer. Rearrange the order. Get high on praise. Make room for warm greetings. Be long on instruction. Hang loose in fellowship and always lead up to God . . .

then out to service. The worship hour must be supercharged with spiritual electricity and wired for practical application. It must operate on the plane of the personal to enlighten your intellect, *and* challenge your will, *and* warm your heart! President James McCord of Princeton Theological Seminary was speaking of the staid, mainline denominational churches when he said: "The current Pentecostal movement may be God's judgment on the more normative churches for their coldness and formality."

Please notice that I said *allow times* for more relaxed worship service. I did not suggest that we switch entirely. Both styles are needed.[5]

Our worship styles and formats must learn to take full advantage of the array of gifts within the body.

Another area of improvement for most congregations is that of the nominating and/or placement procedure for local church positions. In many situations, the program or organizations and tasks are determined in advance and then a committee is appointed to find persons to fill the positions. If we take seriously the idea of gifts and that God has given these gifts to persons and given these persons to the church as gifts, then our program should be based on what (who) is available rather than on a predetermined agenda.

Adding the New

In addition to the old and improved methods, there are some *new* things which must be added in the life-style of the church which would take gifts seriously. The more we deal with the principles involved, the more it is becoming apparent that several new structures and methods are also being called forth. Two of these are more than obvious.

Koinonia.—From the beginning, *koinonia* (fellowship) has characterized the Christian movement. It is a part of its essence. Indeed, before it was anything, it was a fellowship. Jesus chose twelve men from among the crowds which followed him to deliberately create close communal relationships. It was an unlikely choice and one with all extremes. Levi, the tax collector for the Roman government, was chosen alongside Simon the Zealot who hated anything Roman. There were educated and the uneducated, the white and blue collars, fishermen and businessmen. Yet, he called them that "they should be with him" (Mark 3:14, KJV).

At the end of their three-year journey with Jesus, about all they had was a fellowship. They did not have much theology as witnesses. Their question at the Mount of Ascension was: "Lord, wilt thou at this time restore again the kingdom to Israel?" (Acts 1:6, KJV). How they had missed it! But doctrinal theology was not Jesus' primary thrust. It was a relational theology which he sought. Bruce Larson has observed that the Bible deals primarily with relationships and only indirectly with doctrine.[6]

> Jesus Christ came to enable relationships that bring people closer to one another and closer to God.[7]

They had little developed theology, scant organization, no buildings, not even a plan. About all they had was a *relationship,* a relationship to him and to each other.

The apostles deliberately carried this over into the life-style of the church after Pentecost.

> They met constantly to hear the apostles teach, and to share the common life, to break bread, and to pray. A sense of awe was everywhere, and many marvels and signs were brought about through the apostles. All whose faith had drawn them together held everything in common: they would sell their property and possessions and make a general distribution as the need of each required (Acts 2:42–46, NEB).
>
> The whole body of believers was united in heart and soul. Not a man of them claimed any of his possessions as his own, but everything was held in common, while the apostles bore witness with great power to the resurrection of the Lord Jesus. They were all held in high esteem; for they had never a needy

person among them, because all who had
property in land or houses sold it, brought
the proceeds of the sale, and laid the money
at the feet of the apostles; it was then distrib-
uted to any who stood in need (Acts 4:32–
35, NEB).

Thus, W. O. Carver says: "Fellowship or brotherhood is the outstanding characteristic of New
Testament Christians and of all Christians of suc-
ceeding ages to the degree that they are truly
Christian." [8]

What is *koinonia? Koinonia* fellowship is that
sort of deep, committed, caring love relationship
with others. The Greek word has the same root
as "community," "communion," or as in "all
things 'common.' " As one has defined it:
Koinonia is being as committed to each other as
we are to Christ.

> Its brothers and sisters cannot choose each
> other. Brotherliness is not terminable.
> Brother remains brother, even in conflict.[9]

Why is this so crucial as we speak of the ministering laity? Because the discovery of gifts arises
out of the context and in the atmosphere of
koinonia. It is not the reverse. *Koinonia* is a causal
factor. It is only in the context of close relationships with others that our gifts for ministry are
recognized and confirmed. The gifts for ministry
are those things we do to and for others. They

cannot be operative in isolation. Thus, we find their authenticity and practicality only from others. As we minister, others confirm (or deny) that it is a gifted ministry.

Likewise, the *koinonia* fellowship also provides supportive strength for the lay minister. Often we need encouragement, correction, and redirection. This can only come from those who know and love us, those whom we trust.

In turn, this means that a structure of small groups is an absolute necessity in a church which seeks to minister. Today the small-group movement is very much a part of the life-style of the church. It is evident everywhere, both on the parachurch scene, as well as in the institutional church. Most every denomination has some plan or strategy to implement the small-group method today.

It must be said, however, that the idea of small groups is not new. The church has always utilized small groups. William Bangham says:

> During the Reformation, Martin Luther deemphasized the sanctuary church in favor of the Spirit-filled fellowship of small groups which he termed "house-churches." Yet the Lutheran church today bears witness that God's plan called for the continuation of the sanctuary church, as well as the small group. Perhaps one of the best blends of both is to be found in early Methodism. John Wesley required three weekly meetings. Besides

a preaching and a teaching meeting, there
was a weekly class meeting in which all who
attended shared what the Lord was doing
in their lives. The Quakers have been noted
for their use of small groups over the years
and the Oxford Movement of the last century
(known as "Tractarianism," from which we
get our word "tracts") originated as a small
group movement. Many large churches in
this country began as small group meetings
in private homes. Many of our rural
churches over the past two hundred years
have been essentially small groups. Many
still are! [10]

What are Sunday School classes, men's groups,
WMU circles, finance committees, Royal Ambas-
sador chapters, deacons, elders, or choirs but
"small groups"? The difference is that we call
them classes, chapters, circles, boards, or units
rather than small groups or cells.

Small groups, as opposed to these units or chapters, are also different in that they usually involve
a commitment of the members to one another.
One of the principles of personal growth is that
we must make ourselves *accountable* to each
other. Personal discipline is necessary but insufficient. Thus these small groups are usually characterized by a covenant among the members about
personal disciplines and group participation.

Additionally, these small groups are usually
(and wisely) limited to six or eight members. This

sufficiently reduces the number of communication channels to allow participation by all within the group. This participation is necessary if each member is to benefit and to contribute.

Most of our tasks already use the small-group method: we use classes, units, circles, and chapters in Christian education, missions education, ministry, and evangelism. The small-group idea, however, can add the dimension of depth to these. It is a matter of fact that our current program is aimed at the masses and consequently it lacks this dimension of depth. (This is not a criticism as much as it is an evaluation.) If we are to reach the masses, then part of our program needs to be directed toward them in such a way that they can be involved. However, we do so at the loss of the dimension of depth. It is a necessary consequence.

What about those who wish to go deeper and farther? It is at this point that the value of the small group is most readily seen. A small group, with a limited membership to implement participation and with a covenant relationship to each other, can simply go deeper and farther.

Findley Edge says:

> Thus, one of the weaknesses of the teaching and learning that takes place in our Sunday Schools is that so much of it tends to be conceptual in nature. We simply play verbal volleyball, batting words back and forth to each other, or batting concepts and ideas

"across the net." We may discuss how won-
derful Hosea's attitude was toward Gomer,
his wife; consider the problem involved in
Jacob's deception of his father, Isaac; reflect
upon Moses' experience at the burning bush.
We can consider all of these, in a highly
vocal manner, without ever considering in
any serious way where we are in terms of
our personal relationships with Jesus Christ.
In a small group an individual becomes personal. He may be studying the Bible, but
he does so, not in a conceptual manner, but
in personal terms. "This is where I am."
"Here is where I hurt." "This is the point
where I really am having a struggle." The
small group has built such an intimate relationship and such a deep level of trust that
the individual feels safe to reveal the deeper
levels of his struggle which he does not dare
share in other groups where there are only
superficial relationships.[11]

We are only beginning to rediscover the necessity of *koinonia* within the church and in its ministry. For so long we have attempted to accomplish
our tasks apart from fellowship. Yet, the church,
historically and theologically, was a fellowship
before it was a task force. *Koinonia* is intrinsic;
indeed, the church is a fellowship with a task,
not the reverse. The small group allows people
to know each other at such depth that they can

begin to discover, affirm, and confirm each other's gifts; the small group provides a means of encouragement and support as its members begin to fulfill their ministries.

The issue, then, is not an either/or question. We must be mass oriented if we are to reach the masses. But we are also to go beyond the superficial level which is required to reach the masses. The small-group method, with its depth of fellowship and commitment, is the better way to accomplish it.

What are the dangers? It is my personal opinion that these dangers are better labeled misunderstandings. One of these misunderstandings is that the small-group movement leads to cliques within the church. (This criticism was recently made to me by a layman who has been chairman of his church's finance committee for sixteen years. The membership of this committee had not appreciably changed either for that same length of time!) A part of this misunderstanding comes from the idea that small groups are closed. But if a group is to grow in depth, it cannot have a changing membership. If this is understood, then it is not a danger. Yet, as one has put it: "My initial reaction to this objection is simply to say that I think I had rather have some cliques in my church where the participants really love each other, than to have the usual kind of church fellowship where we slap each other on the back, drink punch together, carry on casual conversation, but do not care for one another on any depth level." [12]

Accountability.—A second area of consideration is that of accountability. In previous genera-
tions, the church has spoken of this in terms of
church discipline. This, however, has negative and
corrective connotations. That is, they saw discipline (accountability) as a code of doctrine and/
or behavior which was not to be violated and,
if it was, the erring member was accountable and
had to be disciplined. While this is necessary, it
has proved insufficient. Accountability involves
also the positive and practical dimensions of
Christian life, thought, and action.

While there are many gifts, all the gifts are
body gifts. That is, all the gifts work in conjunc-
tion with the whole church. We are not to operate
in isolation from our local churches or in opposition to each other within or among the churches.
The whole concept of the body of Christ indicates
that we are members of each other and that we
have our gifts to make us useful parts of the body.
It is the body which ordains and commissions
us to exercise our gifts and, consequently, we are
accountable to the body about how we fulfill our
ministries.

Originally, the idea of ordination was that the
body was simply affirming and confirming the
gifts which were already obvious and operative
in the lives of various Christians. The body was
merely confirming what was already a ministry.
While we sometimes make ordination a ceremony,
many times done in the hopes that it will "make"

the person a gifted person, it is doubtful that this was the original intent.

The body calls forth the gifts, equips the gifted, and the gifted one is then accountable to the church.

Dr. James Mahoney suggests:

> Most of all, laymen must have a time when they can "report in" to the rest of the body concerning their activities. They need to be accountable for their service-gift to the body, and they need the body's confirmation. Such a report time should be structured-in at least once every month (weekly is preferable), and the body must learn to respond to each member. For the most part, however, these should only be "news reports"; let the pastor *"editorialize."* Deacons should also be encouraged to receive such "reports" personally, dispensing instruction and encouragement." [13]

The other side of personal accountability, however, is corporate responsibility. If the individual believer is accountable to the congregation for the discovery, development, and implementation of his or her gift in ministry, then it is also true that the congregation is responsible for and to the person. They are to train, support, encourage, affirm, rejoice, implement, and so on, the ministry of that person. It is a two-sided venture.

As the church seeks to develop a ministering

laity, these two new dimensions, fellowship and accountability, are musts. Keep the old, deepen it, but add the new.

As one has said:

> Surround me with fellow-laborers who wish to count for God more than they want all else. Let them draw me into an intimate fellowship of mutual concern. Let them care deeply for me, care enough to encourage me about my potential. Have them take that first step into the vulnerable position of openness, and share about their difficulties in discovering God's will, so that I will have courage enough to be honest about my own problems. Let these same comrades be spiritual enough to assure me that I can really trust God, that he *has* given me a spiritual gift, just as he promised in the Scriptures. At the same time let their love for me be mature enough to firmly hold me responsible for the discovery and development of my spiritual mission. I need them to hold me accountable!
>
> Furthermore, let their love for me be mature enough to take the enormous risk of releasing me to do what I believe to be God's will for my life. And let our love relationship support me with such acceptance that I can risk looking foolish in my attempts to serve God. And let us be faithful to meet and help each other with growth disciplines and personal assignments for particular tasks.

In short, the church must provide a fellowship of earnest believers who will *affirm* my ministry. This will go a long way in helping me to come up with enough faith to risk doing what God calls me to do! [14]

5
THE IMPLICATION
FOR THE BELIEVER

The discovery and implementation of a gifted lay ministry ultimately focuses on the individual believer. The pastor may teach it and be a gifted "equipper"; the church may structure around it and for it; but the bottom line is still for the individual believer to sign.

How does one recognize his or her "calling"? How does one know his or her "gift" and the "ministry" which it affords? Let's approach it in two dimensions.

Daily Work

While we have the tendency to separate "calling" and our daily work as plumbers, secretaries, and salesmen, the New Testament does not. It says: "Let every man abide in the same calling wherein he was called" (1 Cor. 7:20, KJV). This interrelates daily work with calling. It includes both the so-called sacred and the secular vocations according to Paul. If we believe that God creates us and shapes our lives with a will and a plan, then it is he who directs us into the assembly line, behind the sales counter, and to the office.

This is more than saying that we as believers are to use our jobs as a place of and for ministry; those jobs are, in and of themselves, our callings. Thus, there is an ethic involved as to the quality of our work. Carl F. H. Henry states:

> A significant part of a Christian worker's witness is the quality of his work as well as the attitude toward his work. To say, "I'm a soul-winner, but I cobble shoes to pay expenses" is both right and wrong: while Christian witness is always a believer's responsibility, the work he does involves far more than a means of livelihood and carries tremendous spiritual overtones. That he make good cabinets and shelves is the very first demand that his religion makes upon the Christian carpenter as a worker.
>
> A photographer who takes poor pictures, even though he is an effective soul-winner, should either take his vocation more seriously, change his business, or at least confine his witness to non-customers! No impressive list of converts will offset a poor work record; one's work ought not to be of such questionable calibre that it disgraces God, discredits one's employer, and affronts society.[1]

However, this is not to say that one's ministry is limited to the quality of the work performed.

The world of work can also provide an arena for ministry. Samuel Shoemaker reports the story of Ralston Young, Red Cap 42, who holds services three days a week—Mondays, Wednesdays, and Fridays—at noon in an empty car on track 13 of Grand Central Station. Shoemaker reports that "some years ago Ralston Young was brought back to Christ through the preaching and personal work of a minister whose parish moves on evangelistic lines. He wanted to go to work for Christ. For eight hours a day he was carrying people's bags. He began, as he says, carrying their burdens, too. He would fall into friendly conversation with his patrons, watch and pray for spiritual opportunities, and tell them about Jesus and what had happened in his own life. He made many friends in the Grand Central neighborhood, and it seemed right for him to begin a meeting for them. Here, in an unlighted and unheated car, you will find a little company of men three times a week. People have been transformed through that little continuing place of exposure. It takes one converted man, and then another, till you have a nucleus." [2]

A simple formula for testing one's sense of vocation in daily work which has proved helpful to many is: *Be in the right place, with the right perspective, and with the right purpose.*

The Right Place. An important consideration for the lay person in daily work is the question: Is my present job in the will of God? Begin there! Not, is it a good job, an honorable profession, or even an enjoyable one? But, is this "it" for me? Bruce Larson reports of one man's struggle with this, and the conclusion reached is illuminating.

> I know a man who some years ago was a junior executive in a business. He had begun his Christian life by facing up to some failures in his marriage and family. After God began to work in his life by changing these basic relationships, he began to face his job. In a small fellowship group that met weekly for study and prayer, he said one night, "You know, I can't stay in my job. I'm being asked by my superiors to do things that are dishonest. I'm low man on the totem pole and I can't fight it. But as a Christian I can't be dishonest."
>
> We all prayed and for nine months he looked for a new job. He would have taken half the salary just to get out of that situation. But after months of closed doors, he finally said to the group, "I think I'm supposed to stay where I am and let God change the business through me." [3]

Thomas Mullen underscores this idea when he says that "men and women are consciously declaring themselves for vocations that *become* Christian simply because these people *make* them Christian." [4]

On the other hand, it may be that the present

job is not the right one. In that case, the task of seeking the right one should begin immediately, and it should be faced with the confidence that the will of God is the only thing in the world of daily work that never goes wrong. He who is the Way always has a way.

The Right Perspective. Having gained a sense of being in the right place, the next step is to confront our perspective of the particular position: our attitude and grasp of our role. Bruce Larson suggests there are five questions which we should all periodically ask ourselves:

(1) *Why am I here in this job?* Is it an accident or the will of God?

(2) *For whom am I working?* For God or for men? You must "play it" to one or the other.

(3) *What am I working for?* Wages? Prestige? To do the will of God?

(4) *With whom am I working?* God's first concern is always persons. He wants us to be aware of those about us.

(5) *What kind of place am I in?* If Christ is serious about his revolutionary movement, then I am in a place of tremendous importance.[5]

The Right Purpose. Primary among our purposes in daily work must be the conviction that we are placed in this world, and in our particular spot in the world, as "salt" and "light" (Matt. 5:13–16) for Christ. When Jesus likened Christians to salt and light, he did not say we *can be,* but that we *are;* we are *all* the salt and *all* the light the world has! However salty we are, however penetrating our light, we are all there is of it. We are it! Whatever salt and light your place of work has, or is to have, will come from you. Remember your purpose. It is here that we face the really big question: How do I salt and light my place of work?

The easy way which many have found is to initiate a Bible study or prayer group among the Christians and/or the seekers in your office, factory, or with neighbors. This can be done before work, during the lunch hour, or even as brief one-verse discussions on the assembly line or during coffee breaks. This, however, raises another question: How do I identify myself and others as Christians or seekers to begin such a group? Many have found that by wearing a simple pin like the Yoke pin or Fish symbol or by carrying a small New Testament in a shirt pocket or by placing one on the desk, they can often create the occasion for such identification. One may simply choose the bold approach which Keith Miller used in his office. With fear and trembling he publicly announced one Friday that he would begin a prayer group before the workday began Monday. To his amazement, almost all fourteen employees in the office showed up! [6]

A more difficult way to penetrate your place

of work, and yet a most necessary one, is to live a completely transparent Christian life every day. And, when you fail at it, rectify it with appropriate apologies. This kind of life, a life in which Christ is felt to live again through you, is evidenced in many other ways, too. Much is said simply by how one relates to fellow workers, subordinates, superiors, customers, and the day-by-day problems which arise. Even how one gets angry—and sometimes it is necessary—reflects one's true life. The Christian is one who goes the second mile and whose motive for it is transparently Christlike. It is simultaneously an attitude of efficiency and empathy, of concern for products and persons, of personal love and professional loyalty. As Dr. Carl F. H. Henry says: Spiritual talk can never "be an excuse for shoddy craftsmanship." [7] Even one's sense of business ethics is involved; more than one witness has been voided by a discovered padded expense account! [8]

The best way, however, remains the one-to-one relationship of caring concern. One-to-one personal witnessing disallows any holier-than-thou attitude, which may take stands, but also destroys bridges. One must be open if he would seek to bear witness and be ever so sensitive to those about him as well as to the Holy Spirit who is always there to lead.

While the home is decreasingly the woman's primary place, it nonetheless holds forth a vocation for those to whom it is a calling—and a more noble one is hard to find. Dwight L. Moody was once approached by a lady, a mother of nine children, who felt she was called to the ministry. "Yes," Moody is reported to have replied, "and God has already given you your congregation!" All that applies in principle to those in industry and business, in terms of attitude and life-style, applies to the homemaker and mother. Likewise, her relationship to other homemakers is an avenue of vocational witness, especially in her readiness to help, to care, and sometimes merely to listen. Some of the most effective evangelistic Bible study groups today are led by homemakers who see the neighborhood as their mission field.

In the world of daily work, vocation is an option and ministry an obligation. The One who calls us to it knows; remember, he was first a carpenter in the world of daily work.

Daily Walk

The other dimension of calling for the laity has to do with those spiritual gifts through which we minister in and to and for the body of Christ. It includes our daily work, but it is more than that alone. How does one discover it?

There is much in print about the "what" of spiritual gifts but very little on the "how" of discovery. Four of the better ones are:

Lynn P. Clayton, *No Second-Class Christians* (Broadman, Nashville, 1976)

James Mahoney, *Journey Into Usefulness*
(Broadman, Nashville, 1976)

Ralph W. Neighbour, *This Gift Is Mine*
(Broadman, Nashville, 1972)

Rich Yohn, *Beyond Spiritual Gifts* (Tyndale,
Wheaton, Illinois, 1976)

How does one discover his or her gifts?

Believe That You Are Gifted. There is simply
too much biblical evidence supporting the concept
that every believer is gifted for ministry to allow
that sort of mock humility which says, "There
are some who are gifted, but I'm not one of them"
(see chap. 2). In short, Paul says: "Each of us
has been given his gift" (Eph. 4:7, NEB).

It is our gift which qualifies us for particular
ministries. That Jesus called for laborers, not ad-
mirers, is everywhere evident in his teachings.
Gifts are meaningless apart from ministry. We
are to serve.

"No man is worthy of me who cares more
for father or mother than for me; no man
is worthy of me who cares more for son
or daughter; no man is worthy of me who
does not take up his cross and walk in my
footsteps. By gaining his life a man will lose
it; by losing his life for my sake, he will
gain it" (Matt. 10:37–39, NEB).

"Here are my mother and my brothers.
Whoever does the will of my heavenly Father

is my brother, my sister, my mother" (Matt. 12:50, NEB).

Jesus repeated, "Peace be with you!", and said, "As the Father sent me, so I send you" (John 20:21, NEB).

We are to serve Christ and to serve him is to serve others. "Inasmuch as ye have done it unto one of the least of these my brethren, ye have done it unto me" (Matt. 25:40, KJV).

As noted before, Kenneth Gangel lists the New Testament gifts in alphabetical order as: "Administration, apostleship, discernment, evangelism, exhortation, faith, giving, healings, interpretation, knowledge, mercy, miracles, ministering, pastoring, prophecy, teaching, tongues, wisdom." [9]

These gifts, however, are representative rather than exhaustive. Moltmann says:

> Because the different assignments are functions of the messianic liberation of the world, the form they take is historically *variable*. Their number and form can be fixed neither through the myth of a transfigured past, nor through the ideal of an Utopian figure. [10]

While it is important to say what the gifts are, it is equally important to say what they are not. *Gifts are not necessarily talents or abilities.* A gift is supernaturally given not naturally acquired. It is that through which God can speak and minister to others. For instance, as a young pastor I made the mistake of believing that every public school-teacher would also make a good Sunday School teacher. But early I learned that there is a vast difference in being a good schoolteacher (ability) and in having the "gift of teaching." This is not to degrade the work of schoolteaching which may be that person's divine vocation (calling), but it is to distinguish between the two. Likewise, some able, trained musician may sing in a service of worship, yet leave the hearers cold. Others, some with training and some without, can sing and God obviously ministers through it. The difference is the spiritual gift.

> Any Christian could therefore be drawn into a vital, spiritual ministry within the body of Christ, and such a ministry does not depend on natural gifts and talents. Indeed, our natural gifts can even be a hindrance to the Spirit until they are seen as worthless without him, for they encourage a self-confidence rather than a Spirit-confidence in Christian work.[11]

Now, it may be that God will choose to make a natural talent into a spiritual gift, and he often does, but not necessarily. "In principle every human potentiality and capacity can become charismatic (a gift) through a person's call," says Moltmann.[12] Thus, it behooves us to avail our every talent to him. But he chooses and he gifts.

Nor is a gift the same as merely doing something good for God.

There is a difference in doing a good thing and in doing what Christ wants and calls us to do. A classic example of this distinction is in Acts 16:6–10. Paul wanted to go to the province of Asia (from which the whole continent would get its name) to preach, but the Holy Spirit forbade him. He then tried to go to Bithynia but was again forbidden. Finally, he came to Troas in much confusion and prayer. He wanted to preach the gospel and these were unevangelized areas. What was wrong? At Troas he received the Macedonian vision and then it was clear. Christ wanted Paul in Europe not Asia Minor! That was for someone else to do. What was a good thing was not what Christ wanted for him to do. In other words, taking a job in the church may not be the same as fulfilling your ministry.

As Carl F. H. Henry says: "But the Christian's avenue of service is not determined primarily by the question of where he can 'do the most good,' any more than where he stands 'to get the most out of it.' The basic determinant, rather, is 'where God wants me.' " [13]

Finally, a gift is not for personal gratification. Bishop Moulé said once that the gifts are "not to terminate in the ministers." [14] Rather, they are given to be used for others. "It is not the gift itself that is important, but its use." [15] When our three children were small, at Christmastime I would take them shopping for their mother's gifts. In fact, I would buy it for them and give it to them—to give to their mother. Aileen would do the same for me. Likewise with spiritual gifts: they were given to us by God for others.

Thus, the followers of Christ are gifted. This is not necessarily talents nor any good work; it is not something to be used for oneself. Rather, it is a gift for ministry. And all of us are gifted. Believe it!

Discover Your Gift in a Close Walk with Christ. The second awareness step is the realization that spiritual gifts are discovered only in a close, deep, and continuing relationship with Christ. The gifts are gifts of the Spirit which require that we know him and be familiar with his ways. Our gifts and the ministries which they afford us are not discovered in a shallow relationship. As William Clemmons says, "It takes a sensitive instrument to be acutely tuned to the inward frequency of God's Holy Spirit." [16] He adds: "You will never find the depths of the ministry of availability until you make some conscious effort to deliver yourself up in "holy abandonment" to God's activity in, through, and around you.[17]

This means that a devotional discipline is a necessity. The devotional life is that which creates the environment in which the discovery of gifts can be made and it also provides the resources with which the ministry can be maintained. There must be two-way communication between God and the believer if the ministry is to be found and fulfilled. We must seek him in prayer and in the Word; atune ourselves to his voice; and learn his ways of directing us, for his ways of directing us are individual and personal. In short, maturity and ministry go hand in hand.

Gifts Are Recognized as We Do, Not Discovered Before We Do. More and more I am convinced that Paul's experience was the exception rather than rule in the process of gift discovery. That is, he knew his ministry in advance (see Acts 22:14–15). He knew that he was to be the missionary to the Gentiles before he ever started. For most of us, however, that discovery is made known *as we do*. We sing or teach or whatever, and, as we do, there is an inner and outer confirmation that this may be "it." Thus our ministries are discovered not in the closet of prayer, as important as that is, but as we avail ourselves to obvious tasks about us. It is therefore probably more accurate to speak of recognizing our gifts than discovering them.

Carl F. H. Henry notes that "seldom does he [God] disclose to believers their whole biography in advance; step by step he 'leads his dear children' along." [18]

In addition, it is in this journey process that new and different ministries unfold and reveal themselves. What is done in one phase of life as a ministry becomes preparation for yet another . . . and then another.

Look for the Clues. As we seek to discover or recognize our ministry, there are certain clues available to us.

1. *What do you see?*—Jesus bade us to "lift up [our] eyes, and look on the fields; for they are white already to harvest" (John 4:35, KJV), and the Preacher admonishes us that whatever our hands find to do, do it (Eccl. 9:10). It is sad but true that many are missing their ministries waiting for some mystical call while all around them is work to be done. It is a good rule that if no call seems obvious, then do the obvious. It may be that the discovery will take place in the doing of it. Is there a class which needs a teacher, a boys' group in need of a leader, a nursing home in need of religious services? What do you see?

2. *What do you do?*—Are you a teacher? Then, perhaps that may be a clue. It may not, but it may! Do you sing? One young man, a painter by trade, enjoyed singing country and Western music. When it was affirmed as a gift, he sought a ministry for it, and God opened the doors for him to sing and play in a psychiatric hospital, a home for the aged, and in a prison on a regular basis. Your vocation and your avocation may provide clues.

3. *What do you enjoy?*—What is it that you thoroughly enjoy doing that gives you immense pleasure and satisfaction? One lady of my acquaintance, who enjoys growing and arranging flowers, takes the flowers used in the church sanctuary each Sunday and uses them for bouquets to take to lonely people in a nursing home on Monday. What do you enjoy? Another friend enjoyed archery and eventually became the chaplain

for their statewide organization. What do you enjoy? Is it teaching a Bible class, singing in the choir? This may be a clue simply because it fits you.

4. *What do you feel?*—What burdens you? What hurts you when you see it? What renders up an ache when you encounter it? What voids do you wish to see filled? A Christian who had gone through the trauma of a divorce started a ministry group for divorcees simply because she knew the hurt and the need. What burdens you? children without parents? the ghetto? alcoholics? That burden may be a clue.

5. *What do you hear?*—Finally, as you seek your ministry, what do you hear others say about your gifts? Is there confirmation of your gifts from those who are close and honest? Do others affirm your teaching, singing, or service? Do those whom you seek to serve seem helped? What do you hear?

None of these clues alone or all together are proof positive. But they are a part of the evidence. Look seriously. You are gifted . . . for ministry, a ministry in daily work and walk.

A. T. Pierson says:

> Everyone has some gift; therefore all should be encouraged. No one has all gifts; therefore all should be humble. All gifts are for the one Body; therefore all should be harmonious. All gifts are from the Lord; therefore all should be contented. All gifts are mutually helpful and needful; therefore

all should be studiously faithful. All gifts promote the health and strength of the whole Body; therefore none can be safely dispensed with. All gifts depend on His fullness for power; therefore all should keep in close touch with Him.[19]

EPILOGUE

The essence of all this is that all of God's people are gifted by the Holy Spirit and are called to ministry. The church, as Christ's agency and body, is to elicit the gifts of its members, equip them to minister through their gifts through the equipping ministry of pastors, and provide structures and encouragement which undergird and rally every ministry.

At present, such a church is a vision, a maturational vision, but a vision nonetheless. But what a vision it is! In 1974 in my *Breakthrough Into Renewal,* I shared that vision:

> It is a vision of a group of people who are, first of all, committed to Jesus Christ as the Lord of their individual and collective lives and who, simultaneously, are as committed to each other as they are to Christ. (This is the step from an *ekklesia,* an assembly, to a *koinonia,* a fellowship.) It is the vision of a people who have not so much "joined" the fellowship as they have been

"brought" to it by the Holy Spirit because
they have "gifts" which complete the Body
in terms of its various functions. The Spirit
brings them not only because they *have* gifts,
but because they *are* gifts and he "gives"
them to the others. In the vision, the warmth
of their *koinonia* fellowship creates the envi-
ronmental conditions which allow those gifts
to emerge and then the corporate fellowship
provides for the equipping of the person to
exercise their gifts in the ministry of Christ
to others. (This is the step from *koinonia*
to *diakonia,* ministry.) In turn, some of these
gifts are employed within the fellowship in
the equipping and encouraging of still other
members. Some are carried on outside the
church. These gifts, however, are not merely
"good things" to do; rather they are Christ's
assignments. (This is the difference in *lay
involvement* and *lay ministry.*) Some of it is
done alone while some of it is done as a
group effort with others of similar callings
and gifts. The end result is a concerted effort,
in the power of the Holy Spirit, to minister
to the needs of both the fellowship and the
world as Christ leads. Such was and is the
vision.[1]

In the book *I'm OK—You're OK,* Thomas Har-
ris suggests that there are three reasons or incentives to change. One is *frustration:* "There has
to be a better way." Another is *boredom:* "Is this

all there is?" And, finally, there is the *"Aha!"* incentive: "I didn't know there was another way until now." [2] At present, all three incentives are active in the life of the church. There is a growing frustration which admits that there must be a better way to be the church and to minister. There is an obvious boredom, a holy restlessness or whatever, both among laity and clergy. Both are wondering if this is "it." Is this all there is? Where is the power and the person, the joy and the justice? And, above all, we are actually beginning to see a new form, an emerging church. Parable churches, churches where New Testament methodology is being coupled with New Testament theology, are beginning to appear. Aha! There is more! There is a better way!

The conclusion to the story, the fulfillment of the dream awaits, however. The spotlight which has been panning the crowd has now come to rest in full focus on the church.

The next move is ours. Pastors must deliberately enact strategies of change. They must be change agents. Through teaching and preaching, they must begin to share the vision and create the climate for the realization of an all-inclusive church ministry. They must begin the process of restructuring the church program to promote, equip, and enable the laity to discover their gifts and to implement their ministries from within the body with its support. Of course, this is to be done slowly but surely. Happily, it is being done. Reports are available:

Edge, *The Greening of the Church.* A study emphasizing the restructured church.

Girard, *Brethren, Hang Loose.* A report on the Our Heritage Wesleyan Methodist Church, Scottsdale, Arizona.

Haney, *Breakthrough Into Renewal.* The story of the Heritage Baptist Church in Annapolis, Maryland.

Haney, *The Idea of the Laity.* Ideas on how to begin change in the church.

Neighbour, *The TOUCH of the Spirit.* A report of the West Memorial Baptist Church in Houston, Texas.

O'Connor, *The Call to Commitment.* A Classic. A report on the Church of the Saviour, Washington, D.C.

Richards, *A New Face for the Church.* A study employing the restructured church.

Yohn, *Discover Your Spiritual Gift and Use It.* A study of gifts in the local church.

The laity must move as well. Step one is for them to free their pastors to do what God has called them to do rather than what culture has assigned. Then they must move beyond the audience mentality to that of active ministry.

The answer lies somewhere between evolution and revolution. The church will not necessarily evolve into a life-style of lay ministry. Revolution, by clergy, laity, or both is not a certain avenue of change. But, change (growth) must come.

The next move is ours. Yours. Mine.

NOTES

Chapter 1

1. Jurgen Moltmann, *The Church in the Power of the Spirit* (New York: Harper & Row, 1977), pp. 326–27.

2. Carlyle Marney, *Priests to Each Other* (Valley Forge: Judson Press, 1974), p. 9.

3. See this writer's *The Idea of the Laity* (Grand Rapids, Mich.: Zondervan, 1973), pp. 41–43. Used by permission.

4. Quoted in *Priests to Each Other* (Valley Forge: Judson Press, 1974), p. 101.

5. Mark Gibbs, *The Laity—A New Direction,* an address delivered at University of Dallas, June 22, 1976, "Seven Questions About the Lay Movement," p. 27.

6. *Ibid.,* p. 27.

7. D. Elton Trueblood, *The Essence of Spiritual Religion* (New York: Harper & Row, 1936, reprint edition, 1976), p. 135.

8. D. Elton Trueblood, *The Future of the Christian* (New York: Harper & Row, 1971), p. 25.

9. Henry P. Van Dusen, Editor, *Christianity on the March,* "Confronting the Modern World: The Last 150 Years" (New York: Harper & Row, 1963), pp. 58–59.

10. Unpublished report, pp. 13–19.

11. David Haney, *Journey into Life* (Brotherhood Commission, Memphis, Tennessee, 1974, and *Renewal Reminders* (Nashville: Broadman Press, 1978).

12. Quoted in David C. K. Watson *One in the Spirit* (Old Tappan: Fleming H. Revell, 1973), p. 98. Used by permission of Hodder and Stoughton, Limited.

13. Quoted in *What Is the Church,* edited by Duke McCall (Nashville: Broadman Press, 1958), p. 48.

14. *Ibid.,* pp. 56 f.

15. Williston Walker, *A History of the Christian Church* (New York: Charles Scribner's Sons, 1959), p. 81. Used by permission.

16. *Ibid.,* p. 81.

17. Hendrik Kraemer, *A Theology of the Laity* (Philadelphia: The Westminster Press, 1958).

18. Quoted in Clyde L. Manschreck's *A History of Christianity* (Englewood Cliffs: Prentice-Hall, Inc., 1964), p. 19.

19. Kraemer, *op. cit.*

20. Unpublished report by Carl Lundquist: "Enduring Values of Renewal Movement," p. 31.

21. Colin W. Williams, *New Directions in Theology Today: Volume IV, the Church* (Philadelphia: The Westminster Press, 1968), pp. 116–17.

22. Jurgen Moltmann, *op. cit.,* p. 299.

23. *Ibid.,* p. 299.

24. *Ibid.,* p. 308.

25. Hendrik Kraemer, *op. cit.,* pp. 85–86. Osborne and Larson state, however, that "Renewal is a concept foreign to the emerging Church. Renewal implies that the Church was once what God intended it to be and that our task is to bring back that Golden Age. From its earliest beginnings until now, the Church has been in the process of becoming, and it shall always be so. If the Church is true to its Lord, it may never properly say that it has emerged. In both the past and the present, the Church is in a process, moving

toward a fulfillment of its calling. We have nothing of perfection to which we may return; we have no Golden Age to which our deepest longings draw us; we have no plumbline from the past which is adequate for the Church of the future." *The Emerging Church* (Waco: Word, Inc., 1970), p. 11.

Chapter 2

1. "Clement's Letter to the Corinthians" (A.D. 95), chap. 40:5. See: *Library of Christian Classics, Vol. One, Early Church Fathers* (Philadelphia: The Westminster Press, 1953), p. 62.

2. The term *church,* itself a metaphor, is not included here. It is a term meaning "assembly" or "congregation" which Jesus used only twice. (See Matt. 16:18; 18:17.) Jesus primarily used the term "the kingdom of God," but neither of these has any "functional" implication other than "congregating together." See this writer's *The Idea of the Laity,* chapters 1–3, for a more detailed presentation of this.

3. McCall, *op. cit.,* pp. 23–24.

4. Jurgen Moltmann, *op. cit.,* p. 301.

5. Kenneth Gangel, *You and Your Spiritual Gifts* (Chicago: Moody Press, 1975), p. 12.

6. Jurgen Moltmann, *op. cit.,* p. 298. The term *charismatically* here refers to gifts, not to *glossolalia.*

7. Duke K. McCall, editor, *What Is the Church?* (Nashville: Broadman Press, 1958), p. 61.

8. Jurgen Moltmann, *op. cit.,* p. 295.

9. D. Elton Trueblood, *op. cit.,* pp. 135–36.

Chapter 3

1. Robert Raines, *New Life in the Church* (New York: Harper & Row, 1961), p. 141. Used by permission of Robert Raines.

2. *Interpreter's Dictionary of the Bible, Vol. 2* (Nashville: Abingdon Press), pp. 388 f.

Chapter 4

1. James Mahoney, *Journey Into Usefulness* (Nashville: Broadman Press, 1976), pp. 156–57.

2. *Ibid.*

3. Bruce Larson, *The Relational Revolution* (Waco: Word, 1976), pp. 110–11. Used by permission of Word Books, Publishers, Waco, Texas. Indeed, in this excellent book, Larson elaborates on the bankruptcy of most of the "professional" helping professions.

4. Jurgen Moltmann, *op. cit.,* p. 307.

5. James Mahoney, *op. cit.,* pp. 155–56.

6. Bruce Larson, *No Longer Strangers* (Waco: Word, 1971), p. 17.

7. *Ibid.,* p. 19.

8. Duke K. McCall, editor, *What Is the Church?* (Nashville: Broadman Press, 1958), p. 7.

9. Jurgen Moltmann, *op. cit.,* p. 316.

10. William Bangham, *Journey into Small Groups* (Memphis: Brotherhood Commission, 1974), pp. 15–16. Used by permission.

11. William Clemmons and Harvey Hester, "Introduction," *Growth Through Groups* (Nashville: Broadman Press, 1974), p. 15. Used by permission.

12. *Ibid.,* p. 18.

13. James Mahoney, *op. cit.,* p. 155.

14. *Ibid.,* p. 161.

Chapter 5

1. Carl F. H. Henry, *Aspects of Christian Social Ethics* (Grand Rapids: W. B. Eerdmans Publishing Company, 1964), p. 70. Used by permission.

2. Samuel Shoemaker, *The Church Alive* (New York: E. P. Dutton & Company, 1950), pp. 147–48. Used by permission.

3. Bruce Larson, *Dare to Live Now* (Grand Rapids: Zondervan, 1965), pp. 24–25. Used by permission.

4. Thomas J. Mullen, *The Dialogue Gap* (Nashville: Abingdon Press, 1969), p. 87.

5. Larson, *op. cit.,* chap. 6.

6. Keith Miller, *The Taste of New Wine* (Waco: Word, 1965), chap. 7.

7. Carl F. H. Henry, *op. cit.,* p. 70.

8. One of the few books available on Christian business ethics is Thomas M. Garrett's *Cases in Business Ethics* (New York: Appleton-Century-Crofts, Prentice Hall, 1968).

9. Kenneth O. Gangel, *You and Your Spiritual Gifts* (Chicago: Moody Press, 1975), p. 12.

10. Jurgen Moltmann, *op. cit.,* p. 306.

11. David C. K. Watson, *One in the Spirit* (Old Tappan: Fleming H. Revell Company, 1973), p. 83. Used by permission Hodder and Stoughton, Ltd.

12. Jurgen Moltmann, *op. cit.,* p. 297.

13. Carl F. H. Henry, *op. cit.,* p. 68.

14. H. C. G. Moulé, *Ephesian Studies* (London: Pickering & Inglis, Ltd.), p. 191.

15. Jurgen Moltmann, *op. cit.,* p. 297.

16. William Clemmons, *Discovering the Depths* (Nashville: Broadman Press, 1976), p. 35. Used by permission.

17. *Ibid.,* p. 38.

18. Carl F. H. Henry, *op. cit.,* p. 68.

19. Quoted in Jim Hylton's *Just Sittin' Pretty* (Kalamazoo, Mich.: Master's Press, Inc., 1976), pp. 107–108.

PERSONAL NOTES . . .

PERSONAL NOTES . . .

PERSONAL NOTES . . .

PERSONAL NOTES . . .